MUSCULAR SYSTEM

by Karen Latchana Kenney

pogo

Ideas for Parents and Teachers

Pogo Books let children practice reading informational text while introducing them to nonfiction features such as headings, labels, sidebars, maps, and diagrams, as well as a table of contents, glossary, and index.

Carefully leveled text with a strong photo match offers early fluent readers the support they need to succeed.

Before Reading

• "Walk" through the book and point out the various nonfiction features. Ask the student what purpose each feature serves.

• Look at the glossary together. Read and discuss the words.

Read the Book

• Have the child read the book independently.

• Invite him or her to list questions that arise from reading.

After Reading

• Discuss the child's questions. Talk about how he or she might find answers to those questions.

• Prompt the child to think more. Ask: What other body systems do you know about? What do they do? How might they interact with the muscular system?

Pogo Books are published by Jump!
5357 Penn Avenue South
Minneapolis, MN 55419
www.jumplibrary.com

Library of Congress Cataloging-in-Publication Data

Names: Kenney, Karen Latchana, author.
Title: Muscular system / by Karen Latchana Kenney.
Description: Minneapolis, MN: Jump!, Inc. [2017]
Series: Amazing body systems
Audience: Ages 7–10.
Includes index.
Identifiers: LCCN 2016039206 (print)
LCCN 2016039481 (ebook)
ISBN 9781620315590 (hardcover: alk. paper)
ISBN 9781620315996 (pbk.)
ISBN 9781624965074 (ebook)
Subjects: LCSH: Muscles–Juvenile literature.
Musculoskeletal system–Juvenile literature.
Classification: LCC QP321 .K427 2017 (print)
LCC QP321 (ebook) | DDC 612.7/4–dc23
LC record available at https://lccn.loc.gov/2016039206

Series Editor: Jenny Fretland VanVoorst
Series Designer: Anna Peterson
Photo Researcher: Anna Peterson

Photo Credits: All photos by Shutterstock except: Getty, 5, 6-7; iStock, 17, 18-19; Thinkstock, 10.

Printed in the United States of America at Corporate Graphics in North Mankato, Minnesota.

336140804355661

TABLE OF CONTENTS

CHAPTER 1
MANY MUSCLES

You sit on a swing. You push off and straighten your legs. Then you bend them at your knees. You pump them up and down. Soon you're going higher and higher. Whee!

You need **muscles** to move your legs and swing. You need them to run and to ride a scooter. Your body moves and your heart beats because of your **muscular system**.

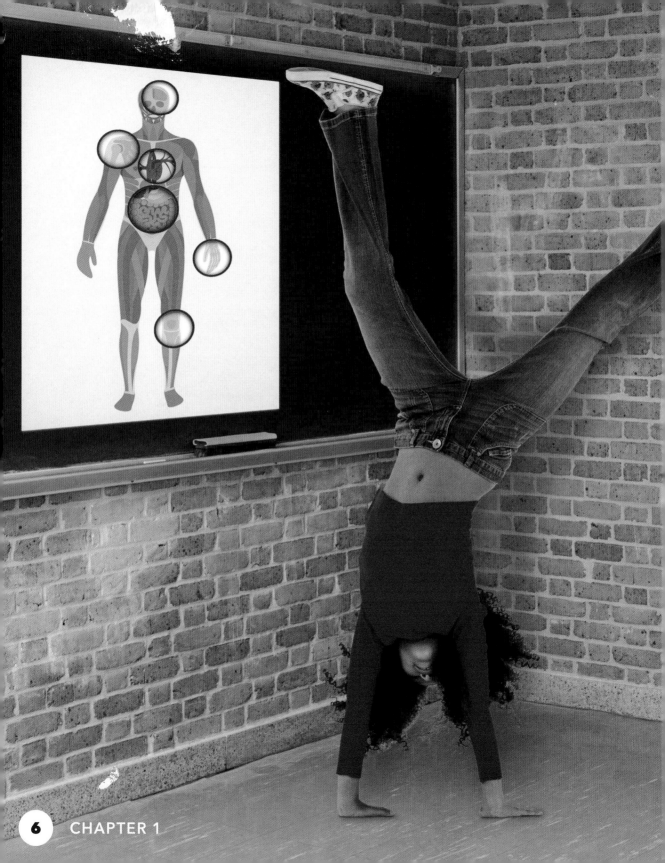

Some muscles connect to bones. You use them to do a cartwheel. You use them to smile. Other muscles help **organs** do their jobs. They move blood through your body. They help **digest** food. In total, you have around 600 muscles in your whole body.

TAKE A LOOK!

The muscular system is made of muscles and **tendons**.

Muscles are made of special **fibers**. They are threads of long, skinny cells.

Muscles work by stretching. Each muscle has groups of fibers. The fibers bunch up to **contract**. They relax to stretch out.

DID YOU KNOW?

Our bodies need to be warm to work right. Using your muscles helps keep you warm. How? They make heat when you use them.

CHAPTER 2

· ·

MOVE YOUR MUSCLES

Skeletal muscles are the ones that help you move. They connect to your skeleton.

Stretchy tendons attach muscles to bones. These muscles contract or relax to move your bones. They make you strong. They help you balance. And they give your body its shape, too.

bone

tendon

Skeletal muscles are attached to bones. They cause movement at the **joints**. They come in pairs. In each pair, one muscle contracts. It pulls on the bones it's attached to. The bones move closer together. At the same time, the other muscle relaxes.

Look at your **biceps**. This muscle is in your upper arm. Bend your arm at your elbow. Do you see a bulge? The muscle contracts to move your arm. Under your arm is your **triceps**. It relaxes to let your biceps work.

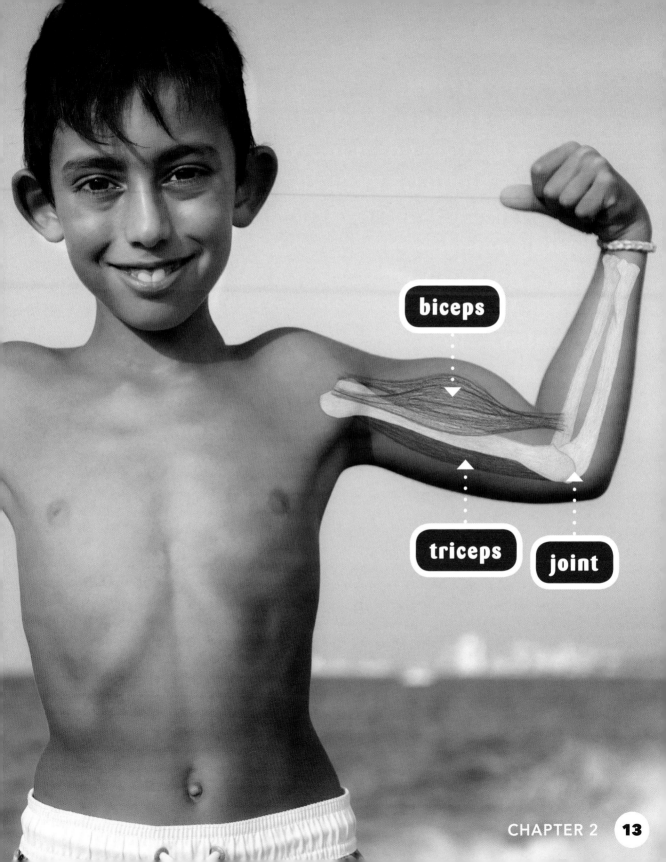

biceps

triceps

joint

How do you control skeletal muscles? You just think about it. Your brain sends a message. It speeds along **nerves** in your body. The message switches certain muscles on. They contract to move. A message can also switch muscles off. They relax again.

CHAPTER 3

DON'T THINK!

Some muscles just move without your thinking about it. They are **smooth muscles**. These muscles are in hollow organs. They contract and relax to push food through your **digestive system**.

They help your lungs take in air. They move blood through **blood vessels**.

Another kind of muscle pounds in your chest. It is your heart. This organ is made of **cardiac muscle**. It squeezes and relaxes with every beat, sending blood to all parts of your body. Blood gives your cells the energy they need to work.

DID YOU KNOW?

Your biggest blood vessels are **veins** and **arteries**. They have tough, thick walls. The walls have layers of smooth muscle. The muscles keep blood moving.

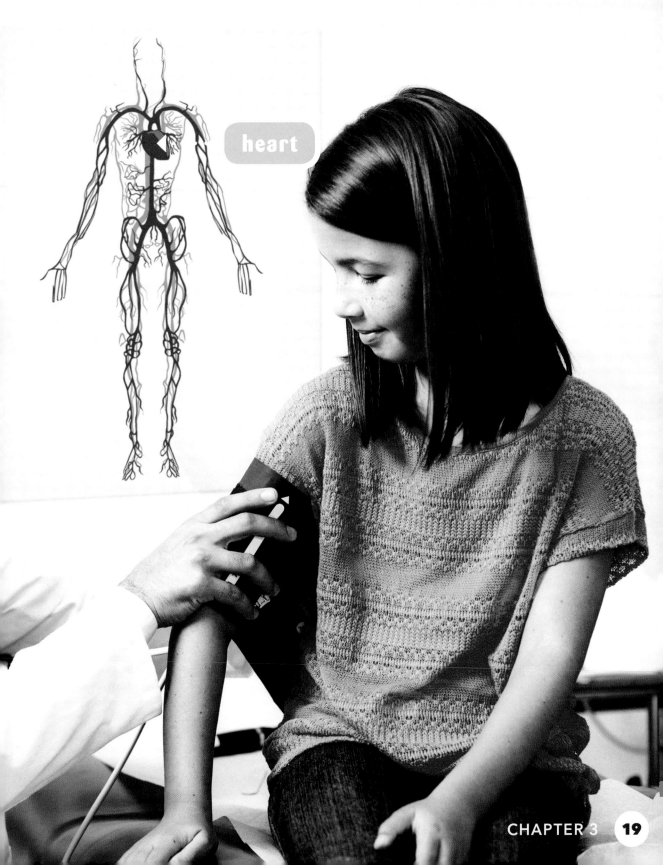

heart

Muscles get bigger when you exercise. Your heart pumps harder and gets stronger. Your lungs take in more air. So go ahead and work your muscles. They work hard for you.

ACTIVITIES & TOOLS

HOW FOOD MOVES

See how smooth muscles move food down the esophagus. This tube goes from the throat to the stomach.

What You Need:

- nylon pantyhose
- scissors
- large plastic egg (Use one that fits tightly in a leg of the pantyhose.)

❶ Cut off the top and bottom of the pantyhose. One leg makes a long tube. This is like an esophagus.

❷ Hold the tube up. Place the large plastic egg inside the top of the tube. Does the plastic egg move?

❸ Now squeeze the pantyhose above the plastic egg. Does the plastic egg move? Where does it go? The esophagus squeezes from its top to bottom. It pushes food down the tube to the stomach.

GLOSSARY

arteries: Tubes that carry blood away from the heart.

biceps: The large muscle at the front of your arm between the shoulder and elbow.

blood vessels: Tubes that carry blood around the body.

cardiac muscle: The muscle that causes your heart to beat.

contract: To become smaller.

digest: To turn food into nutrients the body can use.

digestive system: A body system that turns food into nutrients the body can use.

fibers: Long, thin threads.

joints: Places where two or more bones meet.

muscles: Tissue that connects to bones to make you move.

muscular system: A body system that moves parts of the body.

nerves: Threads of nerve cells that carry messages between the brain and the body.

skeletal muscles: Muscles attached to bones that can be controlled on demand and cause your body to move.

smooth muscles: Muscles that work involuntarily to control organs involved with breathing and digestion.

organs: Parts of the body that do certain jobs.

tendons: Stretchy, strong tissue that connects bones to muscles.

triceps: The large muscle at the back of your arm between the shoulder and elbow.

veins: Tubes that carry blood to the heart.

TO LEARN MORE

Learning more is as easy as 1, 2, 3.

1) Go to www.factsurfer.com

2) Enter "muscularsystem" into the search box.

3) Click the "Surf" button to see a list of websites.

With factsurfer, finding more information is just a click away.